math

expressions
Common Core

Dr. Karen C. Fuson

Homework and Remembering | Grade K
Volume 1

This material is based upon work supported by the
National Science Foundation
under Grant Numbers
ESI-9816320, REC-9806020, and RED-935373.

Any opinions, findings, and conclusions, or recommendations expressed in this material
are those of the author and do not necessarily reflect the views of the National Science Foundation.

Name _____

Draw 5 trees	Draw 3 bees.

Draw 4 rocks.	Draw 2 socks.

On the Back Draw 3 people.

Go left to right. Ring groups of the number. X out groups that are not the number.

3

4

5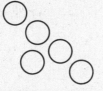

2

On the Back Draw a group of 5 squares. Then practice writing the number 3.

Name _____

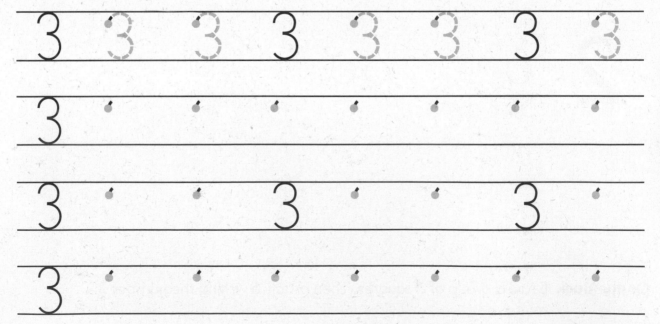

© Houghton Mifflin Harcourt Publishing Company

Practice Numbers 1—10

Name _____

Draw 5 eggs.	Draw 2 legs.
Draw 4 boats.	Draw 3 coats.

On the Back Draw 2 goats. Then practice writing the number 4.

Name _____

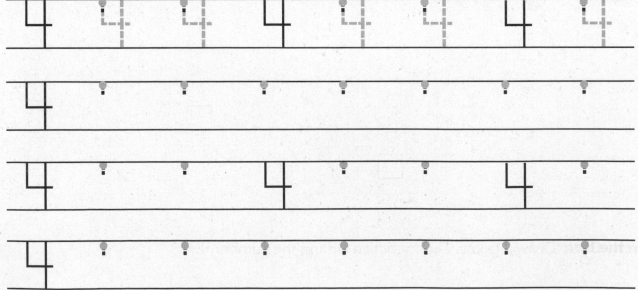

Numbers of Objects in a Group

Go left to right. Circle groups of the number. X out groups that are not the number.

3

4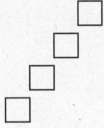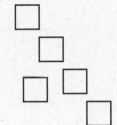

5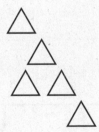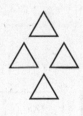

2

➡ **On the Back** Draw 4 rectangles. Then practice writing the number 4.

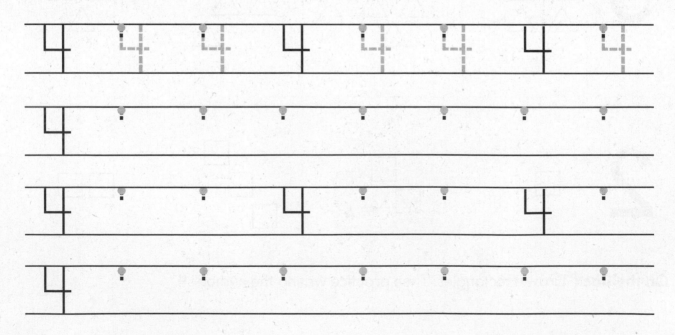

Objects and Numbers Through 10

Go left to right. Circle groups of the number. X out groups that are not the number.

3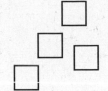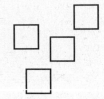

4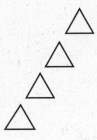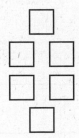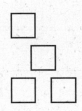

5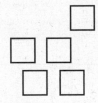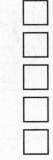

2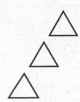

➤ **On the Back** Draw a group of 5 cherries. Then practice writing the number 5.

Name

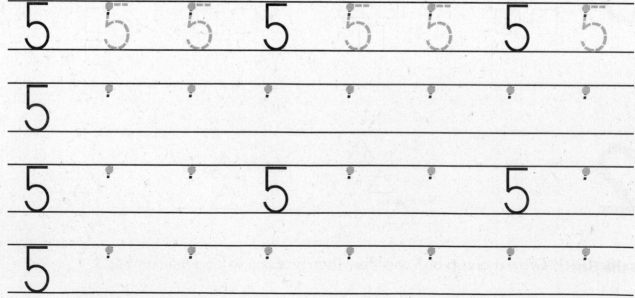

Practice: Number of Objects in a Group

Name _____

Connect the dots in order.

```
   •1          •3              •2          •4


        •2                          •1          •3


   •2     •1              •1     •3     •5


   •3     •4                   •2     •4
```

➡ **On the Back** Practice drawing straight lines. Draw lines that go up and down. Also draw lines that go from left to right.

Name _____

Name _____

Go left to right. Circle groups of the number. Cross out groups that are not the number.

2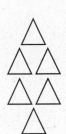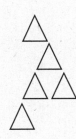

2   □   □□

5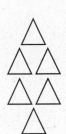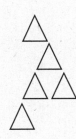

4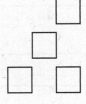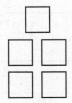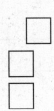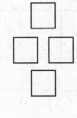

3

➡ **On the Back** Draw a group of 6. Then practice writing the numbers 1, 2, 3, 4, and 5.

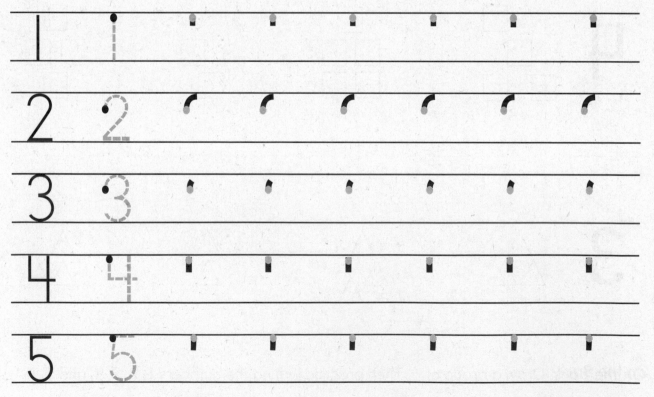

Relate Objects and Numbers 6 –10

Name _____

Ring groups of the number. Cross out groups that are not the number.

6

7

8

9

10

 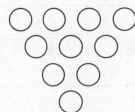 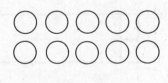

➡ **On the Back** Draw a group of 6. Then practice writing the numbers 1, 2, 3, 4, and 5.

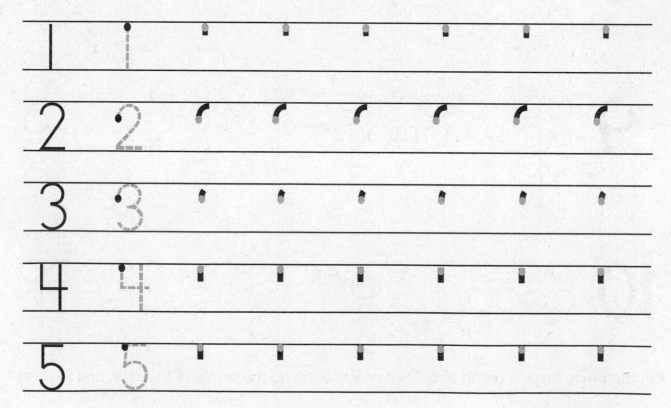

Family Math Stories

Name _____

Ring groups of the number. Cross out groups that are not the number.

6

7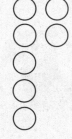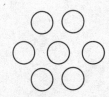

8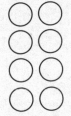

9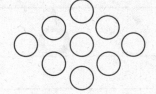

10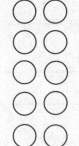

Add and Subtract with Family Math Stories **17**

Name _____

Circle 6 objects from the set below.

Practice writing the number 6.

6 6 6 6 6 6 6 6

6

6   6   6

6

Add and Subtract with Family Math Stories

Name _____

Write numbers 4 and 5.

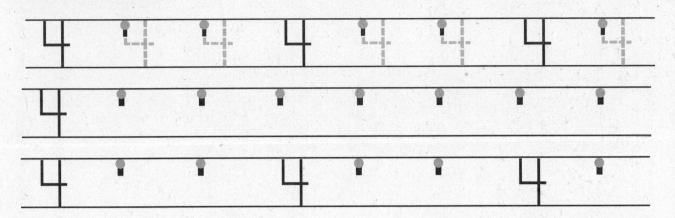

Draw 4 objects.	Draw 4 circles.

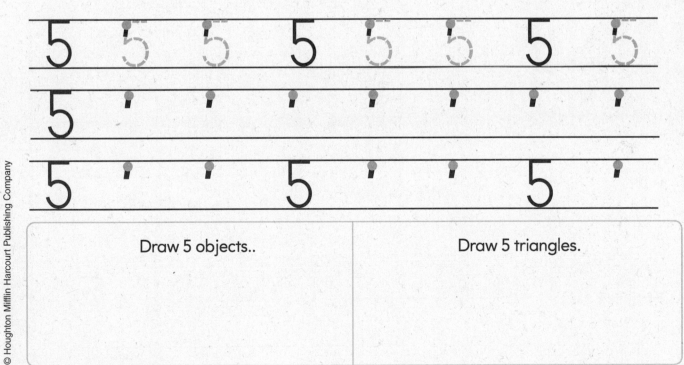

Draw 5 objects..	Draw 5 triangles.

➤ **On the Back** Draw 10 animals.

Name

Addition and Subtraction Stories: Playground Scenario

Name _____

Connect the dots in order.

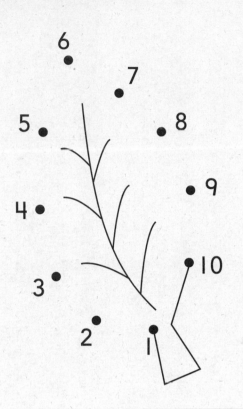

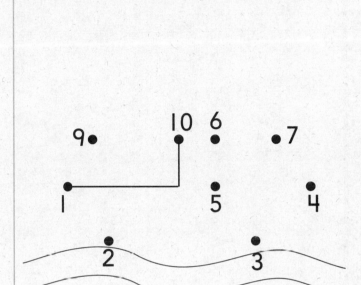

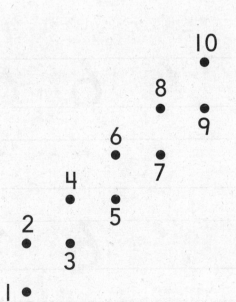

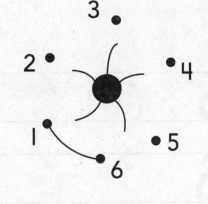

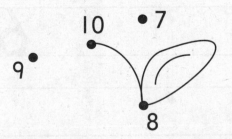

⬡ **On the Back** Draw 6 flowers. Then practice writing the number 6.

Numbers 6–10

Name _____

Ring groups of the number. Cross out groups that are not the number.

6

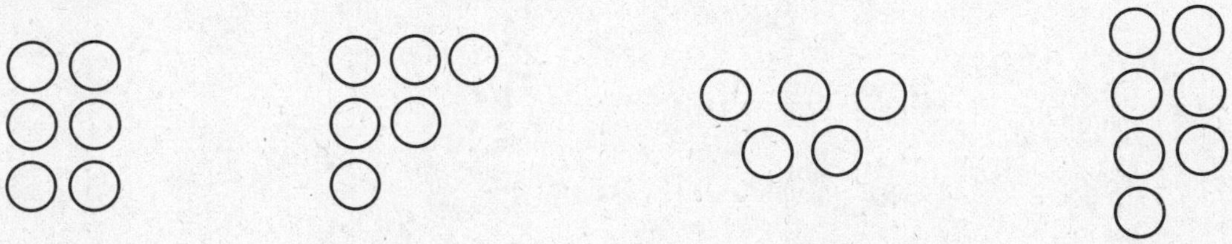

7

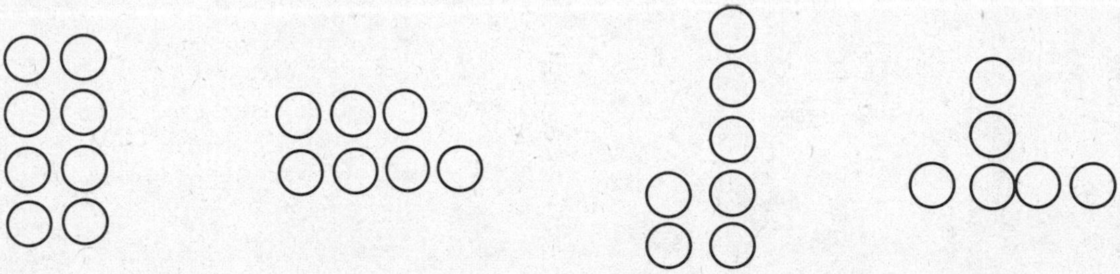

8

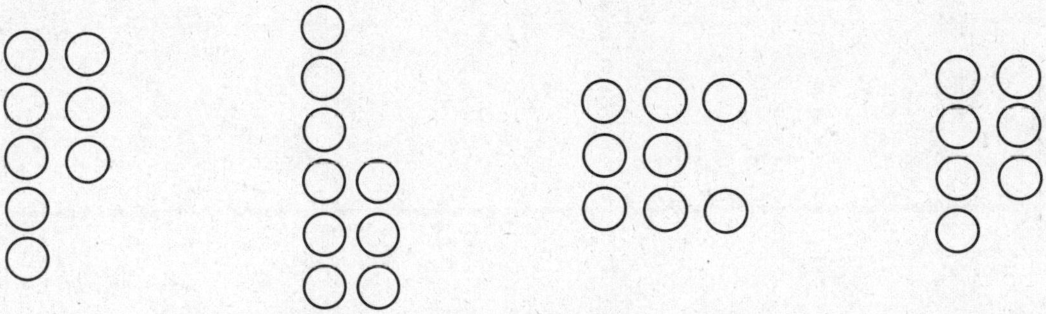

9

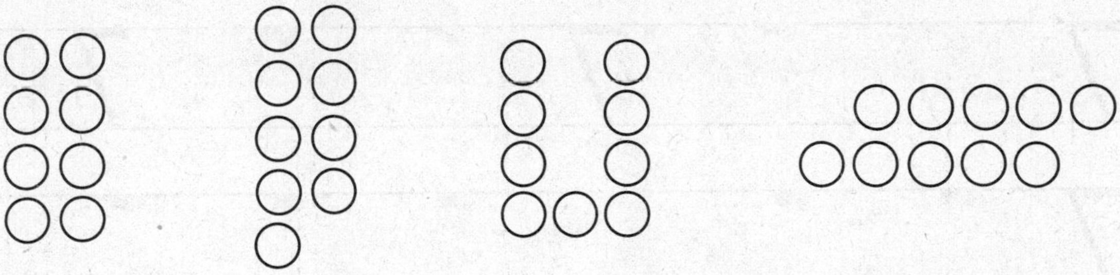

10

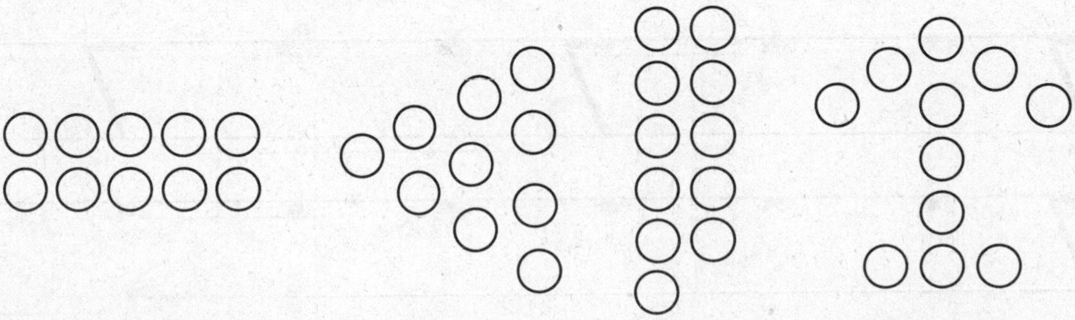

On the Back Draw a group of 7 rectangles. Then practice writing the number 7.

Name _____

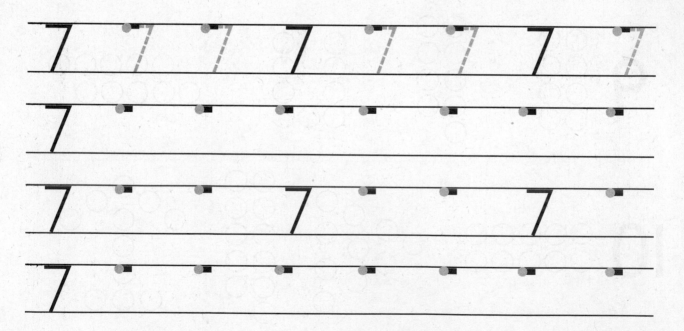

Numbers 1–10

Name _____

Draw shapes in each box to show that number.

5	6
7	8

10

➡ **On the Back** Draw 8 circles. Practice writing numbers 1 through 7.

| 1 | 2 | 3 | 4 | 5 | 6 | 7 | 8 | 9 | 10 |

| 1 | | | | | 6 | | 8 | 9 | 10 |

Practice with 5-Groups

Ring groups of the number. Cross out groups that are not the number.

6

7

8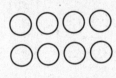

9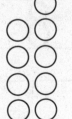

10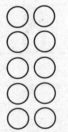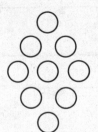

On the Back Draw 8 bugs. Then practice writing the number 8.

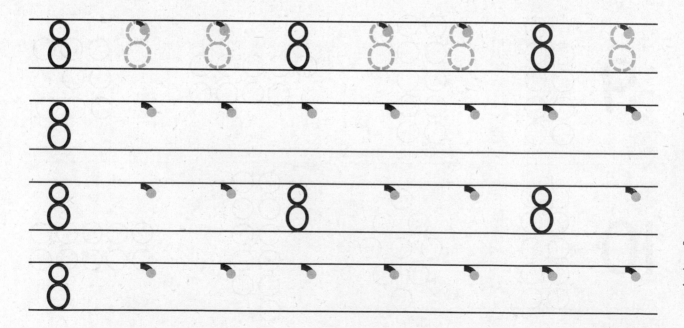

Numbers 6, 7, and 8

Name _____

Use a pencil or marker.
Trace each number 2 times.

| 4 | ● ● ● ● |
| 6 | ● ● ● ● ● ● |

6
4 6
4 6 4
4 4 6 6 4
6 4 6
6 6 4 6
6 4 6 4 6
4 4 6
6 4 4 6 4
4 6 4 6
6 4 6 4 6 4 6 6

Write numbers 1–8.

▶ **On the Back** Draw 9 carrots. Then practice writing the number 9.

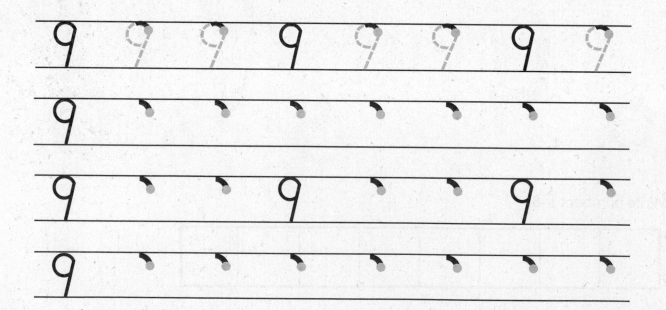

Addition and Subtraction Stories: Garden Scenario

Name _____

Draw 6 hats.

Draw 9 mats.

Draw 7 cats.

Draw 8 bats.

▶ **On the Back** Write the numbers 1–9 in all different sizes.

Name _____

Numbers 1 Through 10: the +1 Pattern

Name _____

Circle groups of the number. Cross out groups that are not the number.

6

7

8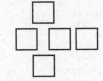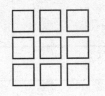

9 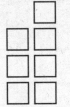

10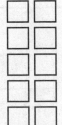

On the Back Draw 9 circles. Then practice writing the number 9.

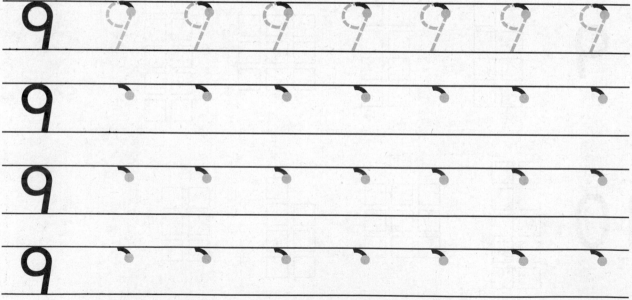

More Numbers 1 Through 10: The +1 Pattern

Name _____

Use a pencil or marker.
Trace each number 2 times.

| 4 | ● ● ● ● |

| 8 | ● ● ● ● ●
● ● ● ● |

8
4
8
8
8
4
4
8
4
8
4
8
4
8
8
4
8
8
4
8
8
4
4
8
8
4
8
4
8
4
8
8

Write numbers 1–9.

▷ **On the Back** Draw a picture of 4 children playing.

Name

Addition and Subtraction Stories: Family Experiences

Name _____

Draw 7 cars.	Draw 6 jars.

Draw 9 books.	Draw 8 hooks.

© Houghton Mifflin Harcourt Publishing Company

On the Back Draw a group of 10. Then practice writing the number 10.

Name _____

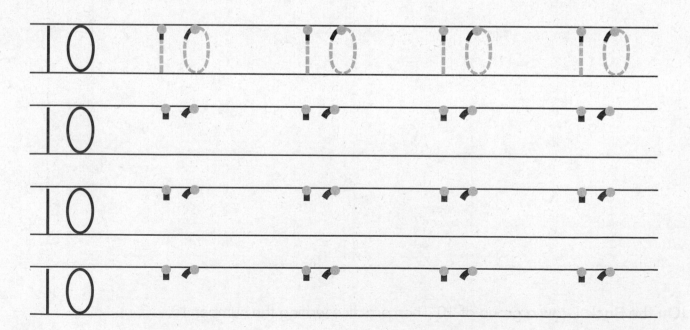

Numbers 1 Through 10: The –1 Pattern

Name _____

Use a pencil or marker.
Trace each number 2 times.

| 5 | ● ● ● ● ● |

| 9 | ● ● ● ● ● ● ● ● ● |

9 5 9 5 9 5 9 5 9 5 5 9 5 9 9 5 5 9 5 9 5 9 9 5 9 5 9 5 9 5 9 5 9 9 5 9 5 9

Write the numbers 1–10.

| | | | | | | | | | |

○ **On the Back** Write the numbers 1–9 in all different sizes.

Name _____

Number Writing Practice

Practice writing the numbers in order.

| 1 | 2 | | | 5 | | 7 | | | 10 |

| | 2 | 3 | 4 | | | 7 | | 9 | |

| 0 | 1 | 2 | | 4 | | 6 | | 8 | |

| 0 | | | 3 | | 5 | | 7 | | 9 |

Start with 1. Write numbers in order.

| | | | | | | | | | |

Start with 0. Write numbers in order.

| | | | | | | | | | |

⟩ **On the Back** Practice writing the numbers 1–6.

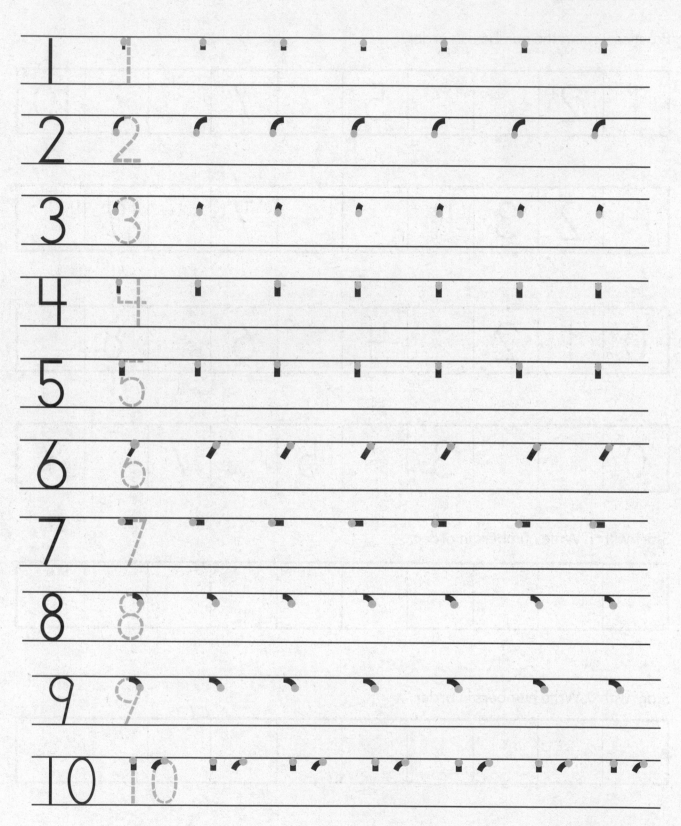

More Numbers 1 Through 10: The –1 Pattern

Use a pencil or marker. Trace all the
numbers 2 times.

| 3 | ●●● |
| 8 | ●●●●● ●●
 ●●● |

8 3 8 8 3 8 3
3 3 8 3 8 3
8 8 3 3 8 3 8
3 8 3 8 3 3
3 8 8 3 8 3 8 8

Write the numbers 1–10.

➡ **On the Back** Write the number 8, and draw 8 trees.

Groups of 10

Name _____

Write the number.

1

 2

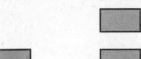

3

4

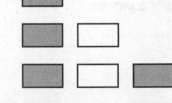

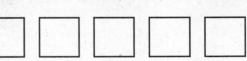

5 Write the numbers 1–10.

On the Back Draw the pictures.

Name _____

Draw 7 apples.

Draw 9 squares.

Addition and Subtraction Stories: Park Scene

Write the number.

1 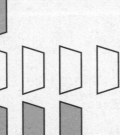   **2**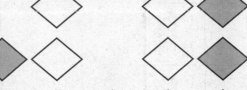

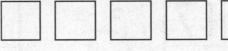

3 Write the number.

□ = (○ ○ ○ ○ ○   ○ ○)   □ = (○ ○ ○ ○ ○)

□ = (○ ○ ○ ○)   □ = (○ ○ ○)

□ = (○ ○ ○ ○ ○   ○ ○ ○ ○)   □ = (○ ○ ○ ○ ○   ○)

➡ **On the Back** Write the numbers 1–16.

1	11
2	12
3	13
4	14
5	15
6	16
7	17
8	18
9	19
10	20

1	11
	17
	18
	19
10	20

	17
	18
	19
	20

						17	18	19	20

More Addition and Subtraction Stories: Park Scene

Write the number.

1 ☐

2 ☐

3 ☐

4 ☐

5 Fill in numbers 1–20.

			4	5					
	12					17	18	19	20

On the Back Draw 15 crackers.

Name

Show Tens and Ones

Name _____

1 Write the number. Draw it using the 5-group.

 = ☐
○○○○○

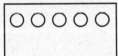 = ☐
○○○○○

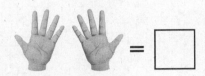 = ☐
○○○○○

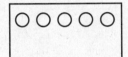 = ☐
○○○○○

2 Use the 5-group. Draw to show the number.

7 = [○○○○○]   9 = [○○○○○]

6 = [○○○○○]   8 = [○○○○○]

8 = [○○○○○]   10 = [○○○○○]

10 = [○○○○○]   6 = [○○○○○]

3 Write the number.

[○○○○○ ○○] = ☐   [○○○○○ ○○○○○] = ☐

[○○○○○ ○○○] = ☐   [○○○] = ☐

[○○○○○ ○○○] = ☐   [○○○○○ ○○○○] = ☐

[○○○○○ ○] = ☐   [○○○○○] = ☐

On the Back Draw 16 bananas. Then write the numbers 1 to 16.

						17	18	19	20

Practice Addition and Subtraction Stories: Park Scene

Name _____

Draw an X over the shape that does not belong.

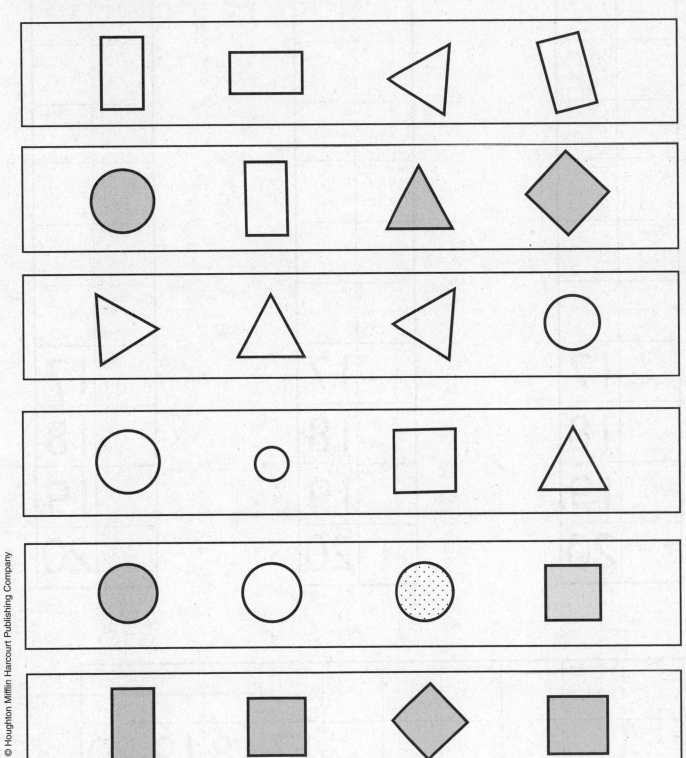

➡ **On the Back** Write the numbers 1–16.

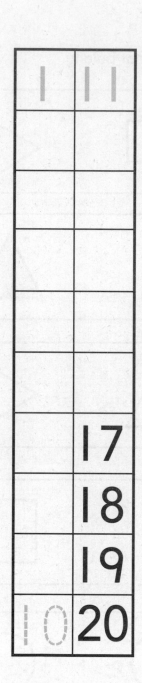

1	11
2	12
3	13
4	14
5	15
6	16
7	17
8	18
9	19
10	20

1	11
	17
	18
	19
10	20

	17
	18
	19
	20

						17	18	19	20

Practice Classifying

1 Use the 5-group. Draw to show the number.

10 = ⬜⭕⭕⭕⭕⭕

7 = ⬜⭕⭕⭕⭕⭕

8 = ⬜⭕⭕⭕⭕⭕

5 = ⬜⭕⭕⭕⭕⭕

6 = ⬜⭕⭕⭕⭕⭕

9 = ⬜⭕⭕⭕⭕⭕

2 Write the number.

⬜⭕⭕⭕⭕⭕/⭕⭕⭕⭕ = ⬜

⬜⭕⭕⭕⭕⭕ = ⬜

⬜⭕⭕⭕⭕⭕/⭕ = ⬜

⬜⭕⭕⭕⭕⭕/⭕⭕⭕ = ⬜

⬜⭕⭕⭕⭕⭕/⭕⭕⭕⭕⭕ = ⬜

⬜⭕⭕⭕⭕⭕/⭕⭕ = ⬜

▶ **On the Back** Show a 5-group by drawing a hand with 5 fingers.
Then write the numbers 1–16.

Name

						17	18	19	20

Name _____

1 Draw circles for 1–10.
Show the 5-groups.

1	
2	
3	
4	
5	
6	
7	○ ○ ○ ○ ○ ○ ○
8	
9	
10	

2 Use the 5-group. Draw to show the number.

6 = ☐ ○ ○ ○ ○ ○

8 = ☐ ○ ○ ○ ○ ○

8 = ☐ ○ ○ ○ ○ ○

9 = ☐ ○ ○ ○ ○ ○

10 = ☐ ○ ○ ○ ○ ○

7 = ☐ ○ ○ ○ ○ ○

9 = ☐ ○ ○ ○ ○ ○

10 = ☐ ○ ○ ○ ○ ○

3 Write the number.

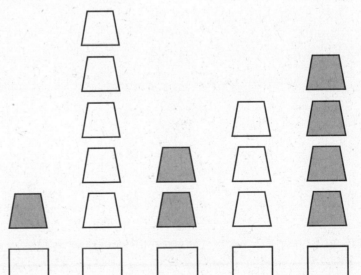

4 **On the Back** Draw 7 different rectangles. Then write the numbers 1–16.

Name _____

						17	18	19	20

Practice with 5-Groups

Name _____

Write the number.

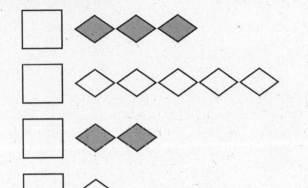

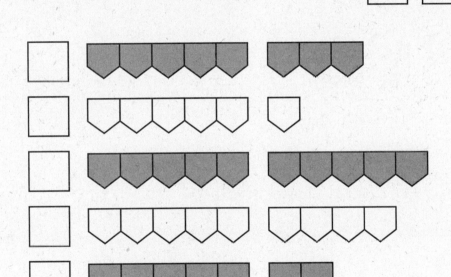

1						7			
		13				17	18	19	20

➡ **On the Back** Draw 14 socks.

Tens in Teens

Name _____

Draw circles to show the partners.

5

⟨⟨ ◯ ◯ ◯ ◯ | ◯ ⟩⟩

4 + 1

5

(empty bar)

2 + 3

6

(bar split near left)

2 + 4

6

(bar split in middle)

3 + 3

7

(bar split in middle)

4 + 3

7

(bar split near right)

6 + 1

⬅ **On the Back** Write the numbers 1–10 in all different sizes.

Name _____

1 Draw a circle around a group of 10.

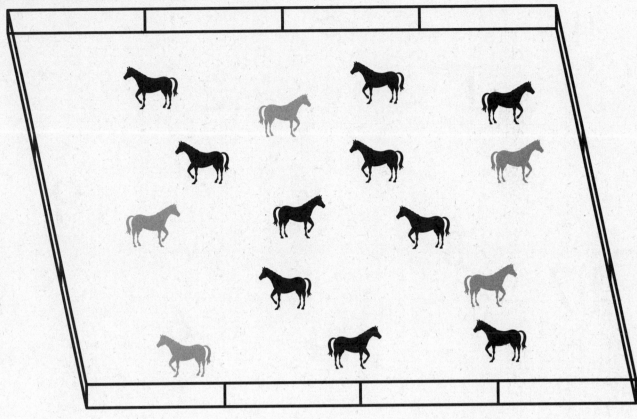

Count how many in all. _____

2 Draw 1 apple for each horse.

⟳ **On the Back** Draw a circle around every teen number.

Name _____

13

4   15

1   2

9

8

17   19

14   6

0   5

18

11   16   3

7   12

Show Teen Numbers with Classroom Objects

Name _____

1 Write the number. Draw it using the 5-group.

  = ☐

⬭⬭⬭⬭⬭

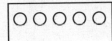 = ☐

⬭⬭⬭⬭⬭

  = ☐

⬭⬭⬭⬭⬭

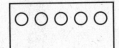 = ☐

⬭⬭⬭⬭⬭

2 Use the 5-group. Draw to show the number.

10 = ⬭⬭⬭⬭⬭   8 = ⬭⬭⬭⬭

6 = ⬭⬭⬭⬭⬭   6 = ⬭⬭⬭⬭⬭

7 = ⬭⬭⬭⬭⬭   8 = ⬭⬭⬭⬭⬭

9 = ⬭⬭⬭⬭⬭   7 = ⬭⬭⬭⬭⬭

3 Write the number.

⬭⬭⬭⬭⬭ / ⬭⬭⬭ = ☐   ⬭⬭ = ☐

⬭⬭⬭⬭⬭ / ⬭ = ☐   ⬭⬭⬭⬭⬭ / ⬭⬭ = ☐

⬭⬭⬭⬭⬭ / ⬭⬭ = ☐   ⬭⬭⬭⬭⬭ / ⬭ = ☐

⬭⬭⬭⬭⬭ / ⬭⬭⬭⬭ = ☐   ⬭⬭⬭⬭⬭ = ☐

⬀ **On the Back** Use shapes to make a picture.

Name _____

Object Collections: Teen Numbers